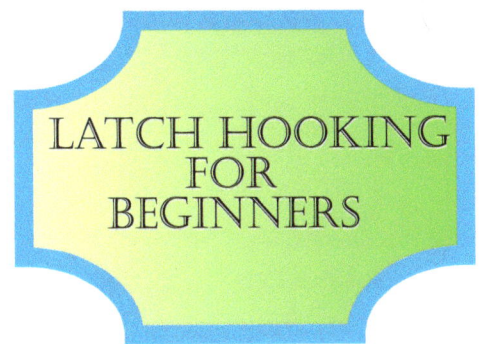

Roslyn Hill

Latch Patch Publishing

First published in Great Britain in 2018
Latch Patch Publishing
Shrewsbury
Shropshire

Text copyright © Roslyn Hill

Photographical assistance www.dianneceline.co.uk
Photographs and design at Latch Patch Publishing

All rights reserved. No part of this book, text, photographs or illustrations may be reproduced or transmitted in any form or by any means by print, photoprint, microfilm, microfiche, photocopier, internet or in any way known or as yet unknown, without permission from Latch Patch Publishing.

Print ISBN 978-1-9993765-0-5
Epub ISBN 978-1-9993765-1-2

The publishers and author can accept no responsibility for any consequences arising from the information, advice or instructions given in this publication.

I would like to dedicate this book to my husband Phil for letting me plod away the hours spent crocheting and writing, and also to my sister Kath who shares my crafting whims and enthusiasm.

I would like to thank Diana for helping me with my images and her children, Lulu, Cielle and Rox for their amazing latch hooking skills. Also for the lovely crochet company of Flo.

I would also like to thank some of my first students, Isla, Liv, Sorrel, Jane and Clare who gave me the inspiration to put this project together and to all the ladies who were willing to have a go at scrumble jumbles!!

I would like to give thanks to John and Rachel for their friendship and support in my publishing journey. Also special thanks to my grandson Isaac for his inventive latch patches, and for his response when asked 'what are you making?' he replied 'whatever it turns out to be'.

CONTENTS

1. Latch Hooking Basics
3. Equipment
7. Tips
9. Chain length bracelet
10. Two colour slip stitch bracelet
    Leaf bracelet
11. Linked chains bracelet
    Side to side stitch bracelet
12. Bobble bracelet
    Picking up loops bracelet
13. Chain Flowers
15. More Tips
16. Pony beads
17. Rings
    Ring bracelet
18. Centre ring flower
19. Beasty Brooches
20. Latch patch options
21. Latch Patch
23. Fancy Yarns
25. And More Tips
27. Bigger Flowers
29. Flower Brooches
31. More Chain Bracelets
    Tunisian bracelet
    Bullion bracelet
33. Necklaces
35. More Necklaces
37. Leaf Motifs
39. 3D Flowers

PROJECTS

 Bracelets

 Flowers

 Brooches

 Necklaces

 Latch patches

 Collages

WHAT IS LATCH HOOKING?

It's fun!!!   It's easy!!!
Anyone can have a go!!!

It's experimental
It's an educational craft activity
A craft for mums and kids
Crafting for disabilities and the elderly
Develops fine motor skills
A basic skill for life
Crochet fit for purpose
An easy form of freeform crochet
An easy form of traditional crochet

It is not rag rugging although there are some fabulous canvas wall hangings crafted by artists combining freeform crochet and latch hook canvas.

Note: A latch hook is a tool traditionally used to make rag rugs and can be found online or in craft stores or haberdashery departments.

Latch Hooking Stitches

Chain
Slip stitch
Picking up loops
Bullion or Spring stitch
Side to side stitch
Tunisian stitch
A slip knot

These basic stitches have been chosen for ease of use with a latch hook tool and are a platform for other stitches to be built upon to make more creative latch patches.

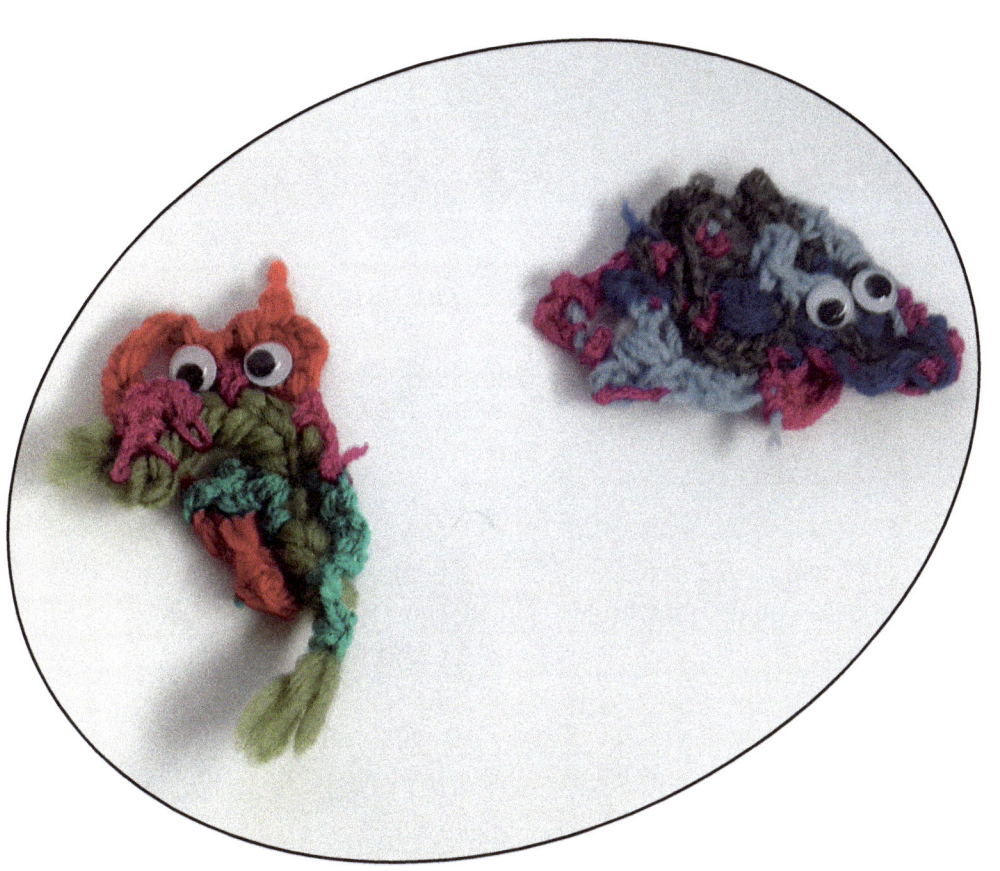

THE LATCH PATCH
A creative, experimental, artful and mistake free scrumble. Start by making your own variegated
yarn and freely find your own stitches hooking in anywhere to make any shape, long, round lumpy or bumpy. Add some eyes and what have you got?
A beasty bird? fish? or dragon?

Have fun!!

Begin with a SLIP KNOT

First place the end of the yarn over the hook and hold with your busy finger.

Bring the end of the yarn under the hook to the right near your other hand.

Bring the yarn under and in front of the yarn that is hanging down.

Take the yarn over the end of the hook.

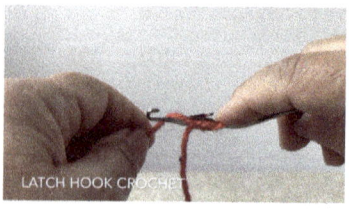

Bring the yarn down...

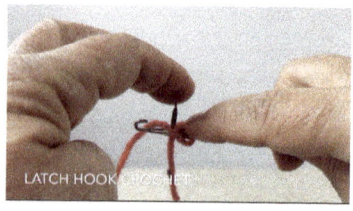

...and close the latch.

The latch is closed. Let go of the yarn with your busy finger.

Bring the loop over the end of the hook.

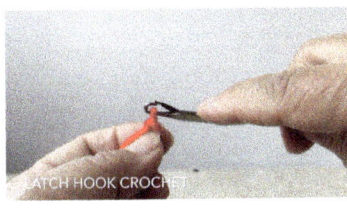

Carefully bring the loop around and under the end of the hook.

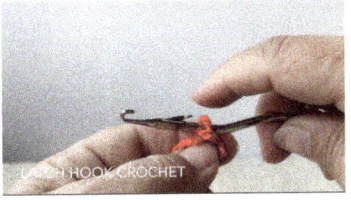

The busy finger can 'do its job' again controling the loop on the hook.

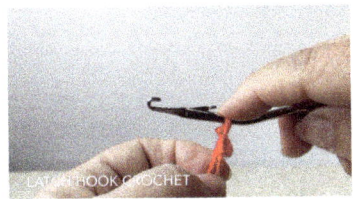

Gently pull on the yarn. This is your slip knot.

Pull the knot up to the hook, keeping it loose.

Latch Hooking Basics

There are four elements to master when learning Latch Hooking.
1. Chaining
2. Making a Latch Patch
3. Projects such as flowers, bracelets, brooches and necklaces.
4. Playtime Challenges

1. Making chain lengths using the latch hook is equivalent to using a hand held small machine tool. It is similar to using a traditional crochet hook, but producing a chain can be easier.

To begin, the hook is held horizontally with the forefinger pointing out to control the loop on the hook. It can be referred to as 'the busy finger'.

The developing chain is controlled between the finger and thumb of the other hand. The developing chain is held directly under the hook and is moved slowly at first from left and right over the end of the hook and back into position. In this smooth movement the latch will close.

The pointing 'busy finger' opens the latch ready for the other hand to yarn under and over the end of the hook.

You may need to pull the end of the yarn at first to tighten the stitch a bit but remember to always keep the tension loose.

Happy latch hooking!!

.

2. The Latch Patch is the latch hooking equivalent of the Freeform Scrumble. There is no pattern to making it. Basic stitches are used to create a small or large patch of crochet and the crocheter chooses the direction and the design.

It is experimental and mistake free learning. The Latch Patch is made by using a set of basic stitches which have been chosen for ease of use with the latch hook tool. These are the chain, slip stitch, picking up loops as in tunisian crochet and the bullion stitch for its textural spring like quality. Later the puff stitch, which may be a bit trickier, can be attempted.

The latch patch is a learning curve and it is not intended to look neat or professional. However by learning to be methodical and by adding the basic stitches, the latch patch can become your own design. To begin with, if your own variegated yarn is used, you are more able to see what is happening in this scrumble jumble. Children can delight in it as the colour changes and they can produce a suprise Beasty Brooch when eyes are added.

Beads can also be included to give texture for added interest.

3. Once chaining has been mastered the resulting chain lengths can be used straight away for a bracelet or necklace. Numerous fancy yarns can then add variety to each project.

This easy method of learning to crochet is intended to open up crochet skills to more people, children and adults. When they are ready they may be encouraged to learn how to use a traditional hook and increase their stitch vocabulary with traditional basic stitches.

4. Playtime Challenges build on the projects encouraging creativity, designing skills and making patterns.

Eleven year old Isla stayed for the weekend on our glamping site (http://luxuryglamping.blog) On the Saturday she was introduced to Latch Hook Crochet and loved it. On the Sunday I showed her how to use a traditional crochet hook and she picked it up perfectly as though she had been crocheting for months! To see her on video see my facebook page 'Learn to crochet the easy way'.

Rox, Cielle and Lulu who are featured in the book were introduced to latch hook crochet and were instantly absorbed. Four year old Lulu independantly made her friend a chain length bracelet at school the next day. Seven year old Cielle soon mastered a slip knot, a flower and Beasty Brooch. Rox designed his own camouflage bracelets and poppy brooch and was so proud to wear them on the 11th of November. Six year old neighbour Florence is 'hooked' too!

Equipment

YARN

Latch hook crochet is inventive and an artform, so a variety of yarns can be used.
There are a lot of fancy yarns on the market so it is fun using lots of different yarns in your work.
However when starting to learn, it is best to use a double knitting yarn and one that is evenly woven to make plain bracelets. Make lots of these until you are well practised in chain making.
Avoid loosely woven yarn at first until you get used to using the latch hook.
Using variegated yarn is creative, easily adding different colours to your work. It is also more exciting if you make your own variegated yarn so you can choose varying lengths of colour. This is important when making a latch patch as it is easier to see what is happening. Adding fancy yarn to this mix also makes it a fun and textural adventure.

How to add yarn to your work

Hook into the place where you want to add yarn, e.g. when you are starting a new colour, make a small loop at the end of your new yarn and pull through with your hook.
Another option would be to tie the yarn with a simple knot and pull tight.

HOOK

The latch hook, which is used mostly in rag rug making, has a bent bar with a plastic or wooden handle and can be bought on ebay for as little as £0.99
You may also be able to find an antique style latch hook with a straight bar and a wooden handle. Avoid the smaller hooks used for braiding hair at first, as they are quite small.
A small traditional crochet hook can be useful for threading pony beads onto your bracelets.

Once you have mastered latch hook crochet, then try experimenting with a traditional crochet hook. Make a collection of different sizes and begin with a middle-sized hook such as size 4mm. Also include a variety of tools to 'play' with, such as a double ended hook or a Tunisian crochet hook which has a stopper on the end like a knitting needle.

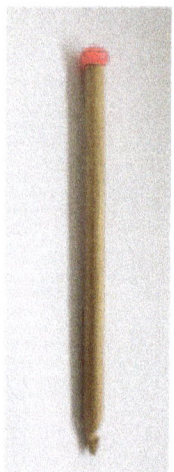
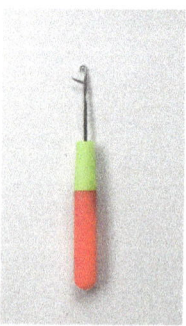

This short bar hook may be useful for small hands.

BEADS

Adding beads can make attractive and pleasing additions to your work. Try to build a collection from old necklaces, thrift stores or recycled jewellery. Note that the size of the bead holes must be large enough to thread onto the yarn you are using. Apart from Pony Beads, beads with larger holes are a bit more difficult to find. Small beads can be used when experimenting with thinner yarns and threads.

How to make a wire needle to thread yarn through small holed beads.

Fold a 4 cm piece of thin craft wire in half over a large sewing needle. Rotate the needle so the wire twists leaving a hole at the end. Thread yarn through the hole and pinch the hole together. Use the needle and yarn to thread small holed beads.

Tips

How to hold the hook
At first take it slowly and hold the latch hook horizontally in front of you at shoulder height. See how the latch hook works by moving the latch backwards and forwards. You may need to open and close the latch hook to keep the yarn in place at first.

How to finish the chain length
Take the last loop off the hook and pull the loop bigger. Cut the end of the yarn and continue pulling the loop until the end of the yarn comes through.

How to make a chain stitch
Wind the yarn around the back of the hooked end of the hook. Close the latch and pull the free loop over the end of the hook and back into place. When you can see what is happening then hold the chain between your finger and thumb and pull the work backwards and forwards over the hook as you are making each chain.

CHAIN STITCH

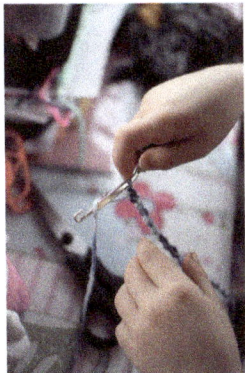

Yarn over the hook end of your hook.

Pull to the left, holding the chain between finger and thumb.

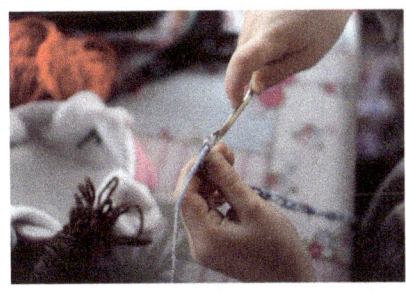

The latch closes as you pull around the end of the hook.

Pull the loop over the end of the hook.

Pull under the hook and back to the right as the latch opens.

Chain Bracelets

Chain Length Bracelet

How to make your first chain length bracelet using plain double knitting yarn.

Hold the hook in front of you with the slip knot over the open hook. Wind the yarn over the end of the hook and close the latch. Pull the first loop over the end of the hook and pull back in place. Continue in the same way to make your chain length.
Count about 25 chain to fit around your wrist. Leave two yarn ends to allow you to tie a bow.

Playtime challenge
If you end up with a very long chain then see if you can chain the chain to make a short thick chain.

Loop Hole Chain Bracelet

To make round loopholes along our chain. Chain 8, miss 3 chain and slip stitch into the next chain. Repeat Chain 8, miss 3 chain and slip stitch into the next chain until you have about 6 loopholes. End with 3 chain.

Two Colour Slip Stitch Chain Bracelet

Make a loose chain then choose another coloured yarn and working into the first chain pull up a loop, yarn over and pull through both loops on the hook.

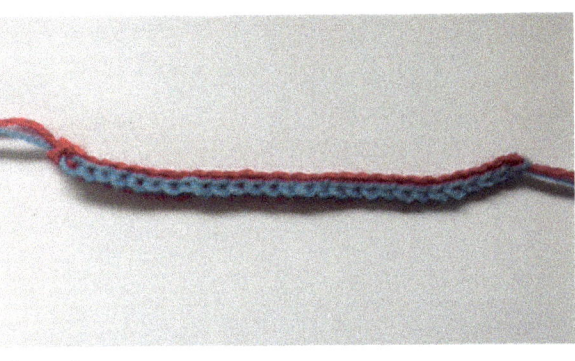

Continue along the chain working a slip stitch into every chain to make a two colour chain.

Bracelet With Leaves

Begin making a chain of 8, then slip stitch into the second chain from the hook and continue making 3 more slip stich back along the chain.
Chain 8, slip stitch 4, repeat to the end. Chain 4.

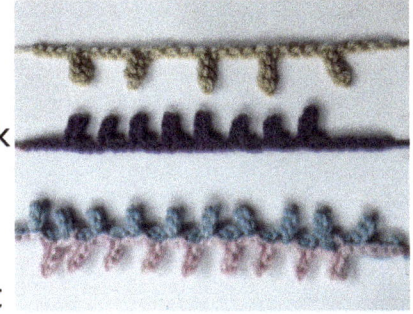

How to Wear your Bracelet

When you are making your chain bracelet leave a small length of yarn at each end so that you can tie a bow around your wrist.

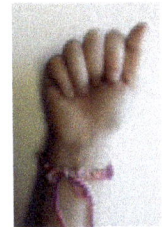

Linked Chains bracelet

Make a chain then choose another coloured yarn and pull a loop through a hole at the end of your chain.
Using the new coloured yarn chain 5, miss 4 chain and slip stitch into the next chain.
Repeat *chain 5, miss 4 chain, slip stitch* to the end of the row.

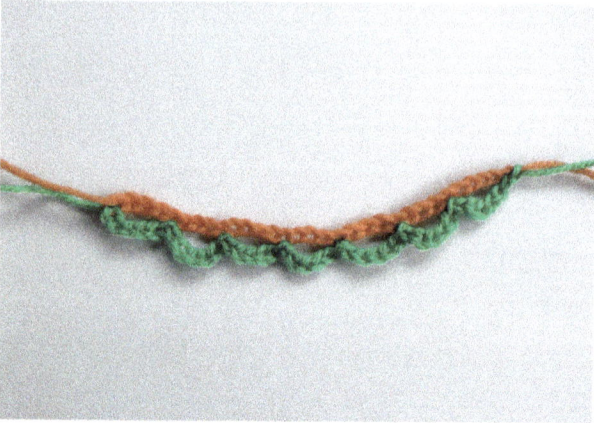

Side to Side Stitch Bracelet

Make a core chain and attatch a new colour yarn to the first chain stitch.
Work with the new yarn making a chain stitch alternately on each side of the core chain.
Work to the end and finish off.

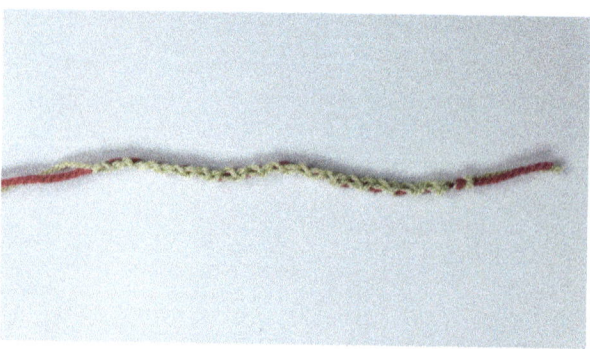

Slip stitch Bobble Bracelet
Chain 5 , slip stitch back into the previous chain. Repeat.

Playtime challenge
What happens if you only chain 4, or 3 between your bobbles?

Picking up Loops bracelet

Chain 8, pick up two loops by hooking into the previous two chains so there are three loops on your hook. Yarn over and pull through all three loops on your hook, chain 5 and repeat picking up the two previous loops. Yarn over and pull through 3 loops on your hook.

A similar bracelet

Pick up a loop and chain one,
repeat twice , yarn over and pull
through three loops on the hook.

Chain Flowers

First make a slip knot with a loop about 5 times bigger than normal. This loop is going to be your centre chain when making a simple chain flower.
Chain 12. Hook into the centre ring again to make another petal.
Work around the centre chain ring making 4, 6 or 8 petals.
Finish with a slip stitch. Cut the yarn and pull through to finish. Pull the end of the slip knot ring to tighten the centre of the flower.
Sew the end into one of the chains or leave them to work with.

Playtime challenge
What happens if you make petals with lots of different length chains?

How to make a Simple Flower

Note : This flower can be made with as many petals as you like and to make the petals bigger or smaller you can make the chains about 8,10,12 or 14 chains long.

More Tips

How to make variegated yarn
Using different colours of double knitting yarn cut lengths of yarn about a metre in length. (Tip: use your body to measure from your right shoulder to the palm of your left hand.)
Tie the ends of the yarn together to make one long length. Take two ends and loosly tie a simple hand over knot, then tie another hand over knot and pull it tight. You can snip the ends short or leave them long. Use fancy yarn too.

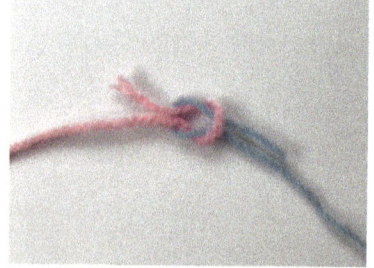 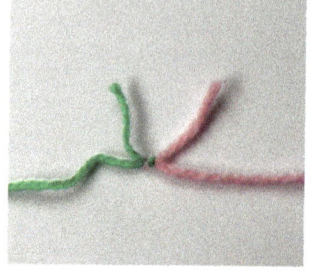

Playtime Challenge
Make variegated yarn with different lengths of yarn, some short and some long.

How to add large pony beads to your finished bracelet.

Using a small sized thin crochet hook, hold it upright and pop a few beads on to it. Then hook the end yarn of your finished single chain bracelet onto the hook and pull through the beads. You may find it easier adding one bead at a time.

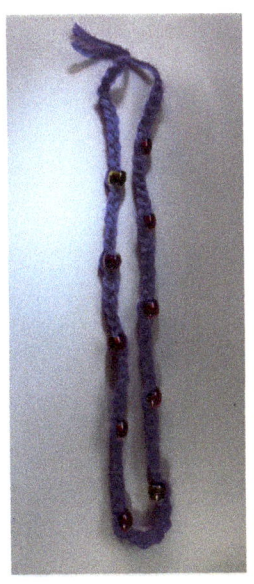

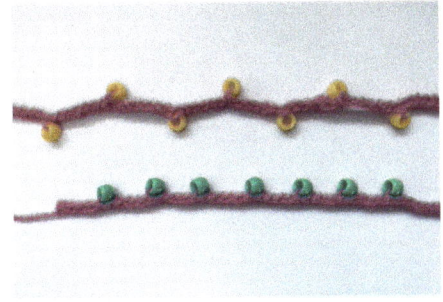

Beads can be added to the yarn before you begin chaining and pushed up to the hook in between making a chain. They can be added at random or spaced evenly.

Rings

Ring Chain bracelet
Make lots of short chains lengths with 11 chain stitches. Tie the first one with three over hand knots. Make the first knot loose and the second and third knots tight to form a small ring. Use different colours in sequence. Thread the next short chain into the first ring before tying it into a ring. Continue adding rings until it will fit around your wrist.
Make about 10 rings and join the last ring to the first to make a bracelet.

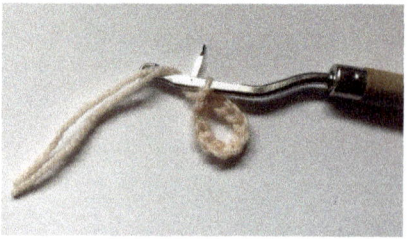

Have fun making things with rings, make hair decorations, add them onto your bracelets and necklaces or hang them up!

> **Playtime Challenge**
> Make rings in different sizes, colours or fancy yarns. Have fun making them into chain link necklaces, add beads to them or make them bumpy with different stitches.

Centre Ring Flower

Make a short chain length with 9 chain stitches using a plain yarn.
Tie this with two or three overhand knots to form a ring.
Tie another colour onto this ring and begin making chain petals around the ring. The advantage of using this method of making the centre ring makes it easier to see the central ring.
The advantage of using the slip knot as the centre ring is that it can be pulled tight to finish.
Tip: Tie the second colour onto the ring next to the join in the ring so that all the ends are together. These ends can become a feature by plaiting them together or leaving them as they are.

Beasty Brooches

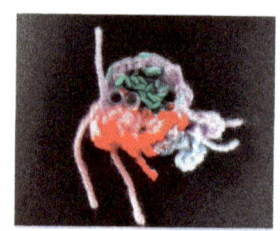

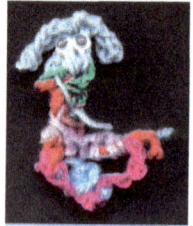

Making a Beasty Brooch

Use your own variegated yarn. It will need to be about 3 metres long.
Begin with a slip knot. Or you can wind your yarn around your hook two or three times and through the latch and pull. Make a short chain, any length.

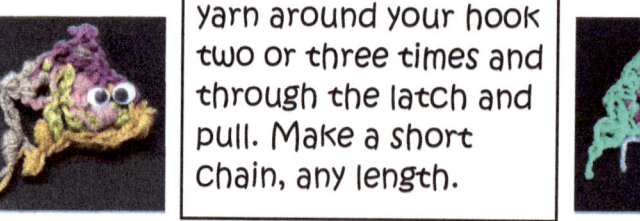
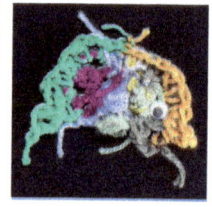

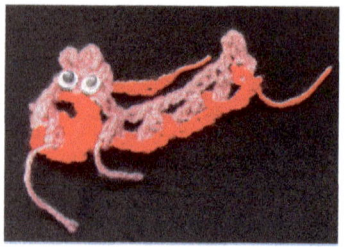

You may then play and please yourself what you do next with your latch patch.
There are a few options.......
................OPTIONS???

a) Hook in anywhere along your chain and yarn over and pull loop through.
b) Hook into the beginning of your chain to make a circle.
c) Make another short chain.
d) Hook into the same hole as last time.
e) Hook into the same hole lots of times.
f) Hook into holes all along the chain.
g) Wind your yarn around the hook before you hook in.
h) Wind it around a few times.
i) Pick up a loop and keep it on your hook and pull through two loops.
j) Keep a few loops on your hook and pull through two at a time or pull through all of them.
h) Dont forget to add short chains inbetween.

Keep going until you have used up all your yarn or add another length if you want.
Add eyes and a pin to make a beasty brooch. You may use premade eyes but you can cut out sticky white paper circles and make a dot for the pupils.
Tip: you can keep your beasties in an envelope and use the sticky flap to cut out and dot the eyes.
Another Tip: If you want a flat brooch it can be ironed with a steam iron.

Latch Patch

Making a Latch Patch

A latch Patch is intended to be experimental and to the untrained eye it may look messy.
However for those in the know, they will never make a mistake for it is an experiment and it will be what ever it turns out to be.

To begin, it is much more fun using your own variegated yarn. It can be any shape, round, short, long, bumpy or lumpy. Make lots and join them together!

Learn what the options are, watch it grow, there are no rules, and you may make up your own shapes and patterns.

Make lots and lots of latch patches and remember to save them all as a record of your work!

Playtime Challenge

After using plain double knitting yarn to make variegated yarn, begin to have fun using fancy yarns and yarns with different thicknesses to add texture to your latch patches.

(1)

Playtime Challenge

Experiment! Frequently use bullion stitch and picking up loops onto your hook. Make your latch patches as interesting as you can. They can be bunched up, lumpy, bumpy, long with tendrils, flat, round or any shape and as big as you like. Add rings and flowers too!!

(2)

Playtime Challenge

Be sure to save all your latch patches. Hang them around your room, see which ones you like best, see if your cat likes them to play with, hang them on your Christmas tree. Wear them as a brooch or in your hair. Join, sew or tie them together

(3)

Fancy Yarns

Use fancy yarns to make Chain Bracelets. Once you have mastered using the latch hook and you have made lots of chain length braclets then using fancy yarns can make your work full of colour and texture.

Fluffy yarns like mohair make flowers thicker and delicate.

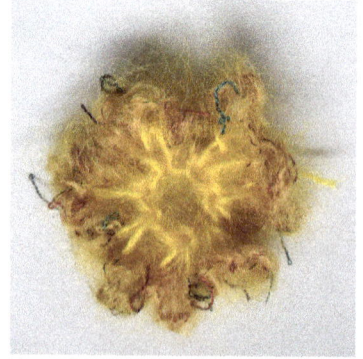

Use fancy yarns to make your Latch Patch.

Use fancy yarns to make a Flower Collage.

And More Tips

How to make a BULLION STITCH

Bullion stitch can add lots of texture to your work.
First make a short chain.
Wind the yarn around the hook shaft 5 times keeping the loops quite loose. Hold them with your 'busy' forefinger.
Yarn over over the end of your hook and pull through all 5 loops on your hook.

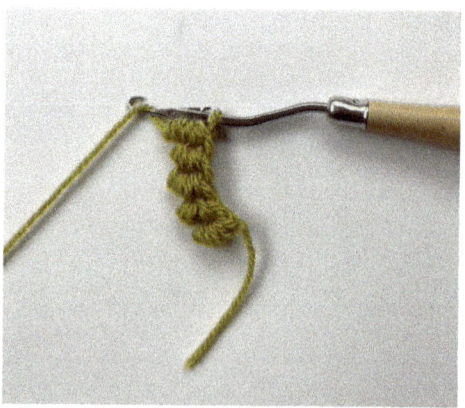

Keep the stitches loose and use your pointing finger to hold the loops.

Add a chain stitch between each bullion and see how they curl.

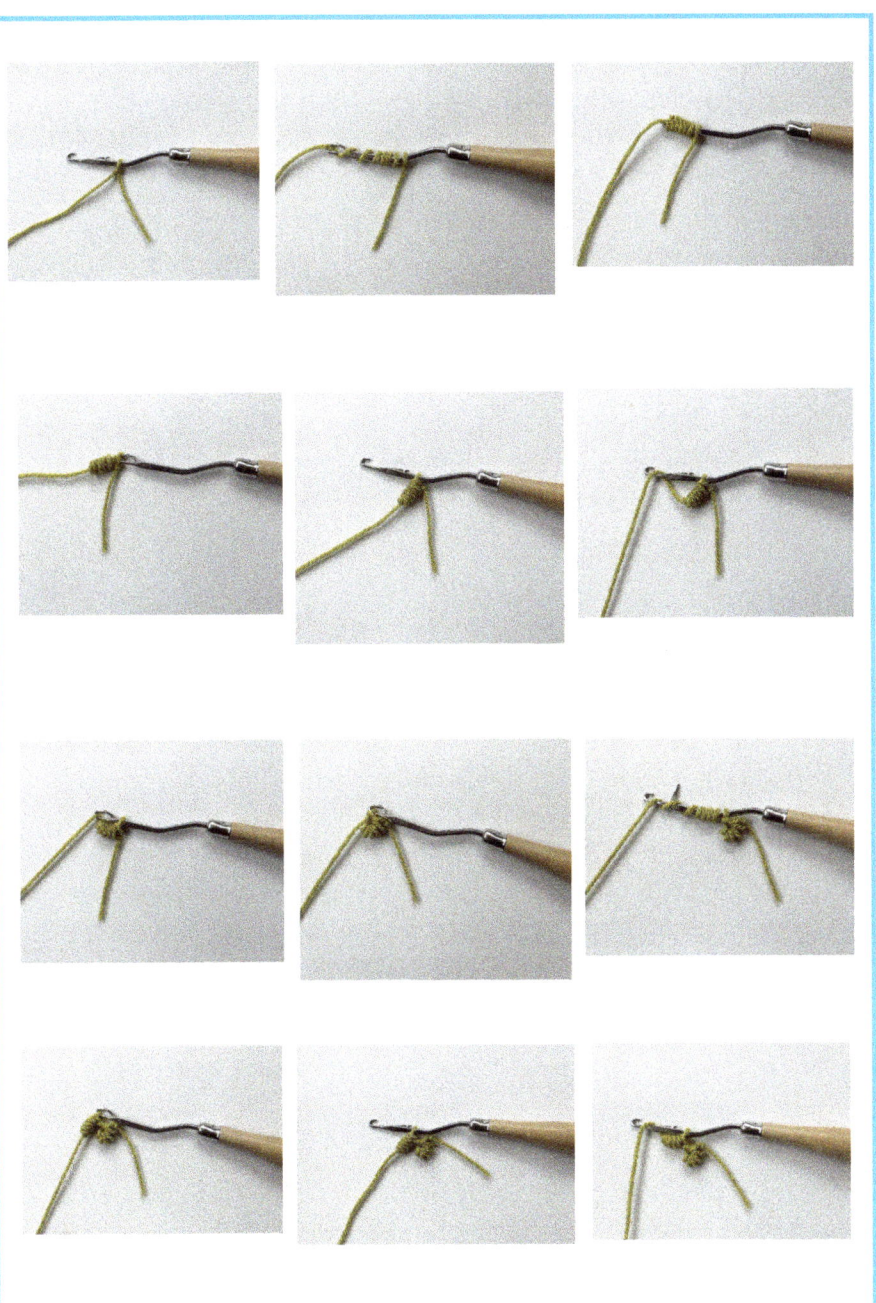

Note: Wind the yarn around the hook as many times as you like to make the bullion stitch bigger.

Bigger Flowers

Simple flowers with chain petals can be made bigger by adding more rows around the outside of the petals.

Atatch yarn in a new colour to the top of one of the petals on your simple flower. Chain 4 or 5 chain stitches and hook into the next petal at the top. It is easier to hook into the hole of the petal rather than to try to hook into the chain.

Continue making chains of four or five around the edge of your flower. Make a final chain into the first chain where you started and finish off.

Playtime Challenge
Add more rows of chain to the outside of your flower in different colours making it as big as you want.

You can be as inventive as you like once you have mastered making simple flowers. Place smaller flowers on top of bigger ones.

Make a big flower, chain about 16 chain stitches long and make a centre ring of the slip knot at the beginning of the chain. Slip stitch into the ring and make another 16 chain. Repeat for each petal.

Choose another colour yarn. Join each petal with a chain and slip stitch.

Flower Brooches

Thread a bead onto a piece of yarn and sew through the layers of flowers. Sew a pin onto the back to make a brooch.

Playtime challenge
Have fun!

More Chain Bracelets

A Tunisian Stitch bracelet

Begin with a slip knot. Make a chain about 30 chains long to fit around your wrist.
Pick up a loop onto your hook from every chain in your bracelet. Yarn over and pull through two loops. Yarn over and pull through the next two loops. Repeat, pulling the yarn through two loops, to the end.
This bracelet looks nice if you change the colour of the yarn for the second row.

Playtime Challenge
Add a another row of Tunisian stitch to this bracelet using another colour so you will have a three colour yarn bracelet. Hook into the clearly seen upright stitches.

Bullion or spring stitch bobble bracelet

How to make a curled spring shaped bobble with bullion stitch.
Make a short chain of 4. Wind the yarn around the latch hook 5 times and then through the hook on the end. Carefully slide all the yarn loops over the end of the hook to form a small spring. Continue with 4 chain. Repeat the bullion stitch and the 4 chain to the end.

Playtime Challenge
Try making lots of winds around the hook to make a bigger bullion stitch.

Playtime Challenge
Vary the length of the chain between the bullion bobbles. Vary the size of the bobbles too.

Necklaces

Beginners necklace
Make a chain length long enough to fit over your head.
Make 5 or more short chain lengths, each one 11 chains long. Make the short chains into rings. Tie three yarn over knots. Make the first knot loose and the second and third knot tight. Trim the ends.
Thread your rings onto your necklace and tie in a bow so it will fit over your head.

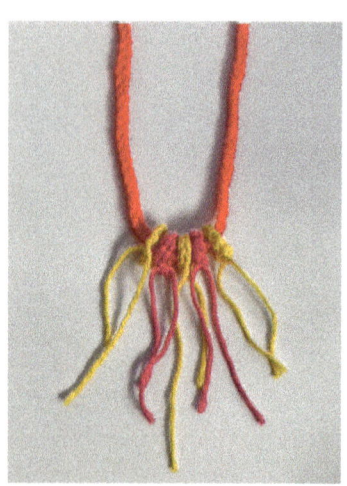

Leave the ends of your ring beads long to make a fringe.

Link chain bracelet
Thread your ring beads through each other to make a matching bracelet.

Playtime challenge

Make a braid like this for your hair or for a sweat band. You can also experiment making a similar necklace using fancy yarns.

Cherry necklace

When you make rings for your necklace, add a red bead before you tie them into a ring.

Playtime challenge

Have fun making a variety of necklaces using beads, rings and flowers. Add bullion stitches and use fancy yarns.

Beaded necklace

Add beads to your necklace and thread rings in between.
Experiment using different colours and fancy yarns.

Bullion Ring necklace.

To make a bullion ring, chain 4 , wind the yarn around the hook 7 times and pull yarn through hook to make a bullion stitch. Chain 4 and finish off.
Tie into a ring and trim the ends.

Flower necklace

Add leaves to your necklace by slip stitching back along your chain 4 or 5 times. Chain 15 between the leaves to make a space to add your flowers.
Make three simple flowers leaving the slip knot loose so they can be threaded on to your chain over the leaf. Add beads to the necklace and tie in a bow.
You can add more leaves and flowers to your necklaces if you wish.

Leaf Motifs

Begin with a centre ring of 7 chain. To make a ring on the end of each leaf. Make a chain of 20 and miss the first 5 chain before slip stitching back along the chain to the centre ring. Repeat to make lots of long and short leaves.

Similarly a bullion stitch can be worked at the end of these long petals.

To make a pointed leaf, make a chain the length of the leaf and slip stitch into the previous chain stitch to make a point. Chain 4 to make a loop and slip stitch along the remaining chain to the centre.

Use leaves with latch patches to make backgrounds for collages.

3D Flowers

To make your flowers more rounded then begin with the simple flower design but instead of making 6 or 8 petals which lie flat around the centre, then continue to make lots more petals.

The more petals you add, the more rounded your flower will become.

Flowers and leafy latch patches can be used to make a collage. 3D flowers can be used too or made into brooches.

If you add a bullion stitch to the centre of the chain when making each petal, it will add further texture and interest to your flower. This can then be used with background leaves to make a brooch.

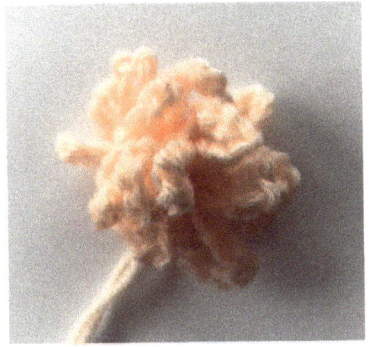

Playtime challenge
Use fancy yarns, leaf motifs and flowers to make a beautiful collage.

Acknowledgement

Acknowledging the work of Sylvia Cosh and James Walters who introduced the inspirational concept of a crochet scrumble and Freeform Crochet.

Welcome to the following groups where you may post and share your latch hook ideas with others:-
Facebook Page: Crochet the Easy Way
Facebook Group: Easy Platform Crochet for Beginners
Blog: https://easycrochetblog.wordpress.com

Email: 4321roz@gmail.com
utube video's: ROZ HILL

The Author

Roslyn Hill B.Ed. studied as an art teacher and is a retired primary school teacher. She has owned a craft shop and dabbled in many crafts over the years. Working with textiles has been her passion, including felting, quilting, weaving, tapestry, knitting, machine knitting, canvas work and crochet, including freeform crochet.

www.ingramcontent.com/pod-product-compliance
Lightning Source LLC
Chambersburg PA
CBHW061806070526
44586CB00023B/2728